Of
Time
and
Love

Of Time and Love

Miscellaneous Poems

by

Joseph B. Roberts, Jr.

Troy State University Press
Troy, Alabama 36081

ISBN Number: 0-916624-30-7
Library of Congress Number: 80-50319

To Enyd
my wife, my partner

ACKNOWLEDGMENTS

Some of these poems have appeared in print before, but not many. Most of this collection is made up of new pieces written especially for this book or for oral presentation at coffee-house readings on or near the campus of Troy State University.

I have included, however, a few of my earlier poems that seemed to please readers when they were first published. Maybe they will again. The earliest is "If Love Be Blind," which was first published in a shorter version in **Personal Romances,** then in its present version in **The Crimson White** (University of Alabama). "The Encounter" first appeared in **These Unmusical Days** (University of Alabama Press). "Restitution," "Sunset at Lowry," and "Lines To a Lost Pilot" were published in **Empire Magazine**. "Jet Flight" was published in **The Sound of Wings** (Henry Holt and Company, Inc.).

J.B.R.Jr

CONTENTS

Reprieve... 1

The Awakening..................................... 2

Fruition... 3

In the Absence of Love............................ 4

Episode.. 5

Forbidden Flight.................................. 6

Familiar Tune..................................... 7

Excerpts From **The How-To-Love Book**........... 8

If Love Be Blind.................................. 9

False Start....................................... 11

Restitution....................................... 12

After Your Leaving................................ 13

The Wanderer Speaks............................... 14

There Is a Black Bird Yonder...................... 15

Nemesis... 16

Haiku Patterns.................................... 17

Fly Quick the Dove................................ 18

To August H. Mason—Esteemed Teacher........... 19

The Encounter..................................... 20

Sunset at Lowry................................... 21

Jet Flight.. 22

Lines To a Lost Pilot............................. 23

Evening Song No More.............................. 24

Overseas Diary.................................... 25

A Letter Never Written............................ 28

An Incident of Spring............................. 29

Letter To the Editor.............................. 31

My Father Died Laughing.........................33

Overheard in the Lobby
      Between Double Features....................35

It'll Probably Be Like That.......................36

Handy Snack....................................37

Summer Cruise..................................38

My Catch.......................................39

Genesis III......................................41

Three Coeds Walk Abreast.......................42

Identity...43

Story on Page 12................................45

The Reward....................................47

A Trap Untended................................50

He Spent Too Long..............................51

Siesta..52

On Reflection..................................53

Odysseus To Penelope..........................55

The Promise...................................56

In Answer To Your Question....................58

Closing Scene..................................59

Of Time and Love

Reprieve

I should write only elegies.
My Proustian days are crowded
With unkept promises and lost chances,
A round of melodies from old productions
Played in an empty hall,
And I see how the years mount up
With memories of final acts,
Closing scenes, curtain lines.
I know now the risk of living
In a world of mortals
And the uncertainties of tomorrow.
But I think of you—
Your fresh smile,
Your quick hunger,
Your bright strength,
Your courage to dare to be
Who you are—
And my old muse once more
Sings love songs.

The Awakening

That morning
While you lay in soft sleep
I watched the rhythm
Of your undulating breasts
And thought of the quick tides
Rising and falling
With the eternal moons
And the ageless seas running
As the blood flows
Through your veins
From your pumping heart
Outward and back.
Then I thought
How mortal and brief
Was our little world
And I hurried
To awake you.

Fruition

Caused by his leaving
Pain enough to want again
What she had given,
She reached out from the dark bed
Of her loneliness
To grasp what was not there.

She caught instead
A flutter of whispered vows
Spoken quickly in the toss of sound
And the thrash of memories—
Then the quiet.

She clutched herself, then felt
The word, once delicate, casual,
Hardly noticed at all,
Suddenly move in her
And kick its feet against her heart.

In the Absence of Love

Here in this quiet room
Her mind flits from dream to dream
Like a nest-building bird
Carrying fragments of memories
To shape her hope of love
Hopping across a lawn of green years
Dragging snatches of song and laughter
Then up in flight to swaying bough
To build a place for them
In hope of one more spring
But evening comes again
And with the dark a cold wind rises
Telling her winter remains
And no birds fly.

Episode

That day at summer beach
We made time complete
Before—then—after
To that cottage of
Someone else's yesterdays
We brought our bright moments
Of anticipation
Those promised pleasures
Cherished from our first meeting
Took them to bed with us
And discovered that excruciating pause
The stop of heart beat and breath
While the pulse of time
Pushed us out to sea
Then we knew what "after" meant
And the crazy swirl of life
Caught us in its lazy current
Sent us floating, drifting
On a transient swell of love
And washed us—helpless—
Toward the inevitable shore.

Forbidden Flight

They cling flesh to flesh as an infant monkey to its mother
    Swinging through an alien forest
The fear of falling always there in the clandestine dark
    They clutch breasts to breasts, her face
    So close to his her whisper brushes
        Breathful against his lips,
          "Hold me."
And his dreading eyes shut tight as if to block out
    The vision of slender branches bending
        Beneath their too heavy weight—
          "Hold me!"
He feels their naked bodies slide down the yielding limb
    Toppling, turning in the careless air
    He cannot catch his breath to cry alarm
        They crash
    They shake the shocked earth with impact
        Collapse inside
    The wounds of their asundered passion
    Not in the bodies prone on black earth
    But in the hearts splintered, the lungs played out
      They lie spent, shattered, apart
        Forever separated.

Familiar Tune

According to a televised report
(Very scientific, even showed the clay tablets),
Some 1500 years before the birth of Christ
Somebody wrote a song
Words and music (for lyre).
The archaeologist who found it was a woman,
Bright and chic but scholarly.
She said it took her fifteen years
To figure out the words and melody,
Time well spent, she thought.
She played it for us on television.
It sounded sort of lonesome, sad, hurting.
I wasn't surprised when she said
It was a love song.

Excerpts From THE HOW-TO-LOVE BOOK

How to gain love:
  Give it.

How to know love:
  Feel it.

How to enjoy love:
  Accept it.

How to lose love:
  Pursue it.

How to keep love:
  Free it.

How to kill love:
  Demand it.

How to show love:
  Live it.

How to make love:
  Practice it.

How to increase love:
  Share it.

How to speak love:
  Be it.

If Love Be Blind

If love be blind
Then why, my dear,
Should vision come
So sharp and clear

To me whose eyes
Had never seen
How purple grapes
With leaves of green

Could clustered hang
From bending bough,
How sleek, black horse
And red-patched cow

Could pastured graze
Across sweet land,
Swept clean and pure
By God's own hand?

If love makes blind
The eye, my dear,
Then does it not
Make deaf the ear?

But I have heard
The bleating goat,
The grunting sow,
The squealing shoat,

The whistling bird,
The crowing cock,
The sighing wind,
The silent rock—

All music that
I never heard
Until your love,
Like magic word,

Bestowed the gift
Of life on me,
With ear to hear
And eye to see

Before your love
So freed my mind,
I was deaf—
And numb—and blind.

False Start

I went in search of beauty
When spring first filled the air,
But the jonquil stalks were budless
And the apple boughs were bare.

The mud from melting snow
Had stained the lawn with red
And covered all the violets
In my washed-out flower bed.

So, like the sleepy groundhog
Who sees his shadow black,
I went into my winter home
And turned the calendar back.

Restitution

Turn back the china clock to time
Before when temptation stood
Outside and waited for little boys
Who ran off to the wood
Instead of doing chores they should.

Push back the kitchen door and see
How once in our house Good
Sat tabled with my father and
Did what she could
To make life happy; and it was.

Hold back the door and let me slip
Back through to home, and then
Shut tight the door before the Evil
Can follow me back in
From that black wood where I have been.

After Your Leaving

Lost one, this road you led me on is long
And I am tired from walking in its dust;
The wind is chilled and moans in mournful song
Through bloomless bushes, half leafless from rust;
And I have many miles to walk without
Your hand to guide me along the twisting route
And point the distant star for my searching eye.

Now breathe I deeply the dead, cold air
And hear the dry leaves rustling drearily
And see those lost dreams, left lying bare
Along the rutted road; and wearily
I wander, emptied of thought by pain,
Knowing only that you are gone and rain
Falls on my cheeks from a cloudless sky.

The Wanderer Speaks

If you can learn from seeing,
　　Look into my eyes.
Read the sorrow of my searching;
　　Look deeply and grow wise.

There Is a Black Bird Yonder

There is a black bird yonder—
I feel his burning eyes on me.
He knows how close am I,
But I know not how close is he.

Nemesis

In the pool of our dreams we go wading,
    Always looking down.
We laugh at reflections breaking there,
    But we wade too deep, and we drown.

Haiku Patterns

They sing no songs,
The rabbit in my garden
And the white gardenia.

* * *

In ecstasy a moth
Dances in the lantern light—
Then the flame.

* * *

Across the river
Sunbeams slant through slate gray clouds,
Ignoring thunder.

* * *

Beneath the summer moon
A nightingale sings,
Caring not who listens.

Fly Quick the Dove

Release the dove, old man,
Before the sun's fast setting
Can steal another day.
Open wide the wicker cage—
Tomorrow has been served enough
By patient waiting.
Send out the soft plumed messenger
To dot the sky with joyful flight,
Return with leaf in beak,
Life's green token.

Look to the land receding waters give;
From those muddy hills must come
The fields made verdant by your toil,
The reed-thatched shelter for your brood,
The fire heaped high and hot again,
The woman heavy with your seed.
You have a world to build
With the sweat of your labor and your bed.

How high are the waters now?
Time is running out, old man.
Fly quick the dove.

To August H. Mason
Esteemed Teacher

Your scintillating mind
Was not yours alone.
Your electric thoughts
Became ours too.

Your shining words
Quickened our blossoms.
Sun ripened, the fruit fell
At your feet.

The Encounter

The waysider sat and with patient hammer
Cracked the stubborn hickory nuts,
Dug into the unyielding shells
With a penknife blade to get
Fragments of the meats,
Hardly enough to tip his tongue.
I paused beside him from my walk,
Snapped peanut shells between my fingers,
Popped the brittle nuts into my mouth.
"Here," I said, "try some of these."
He shook his head and dug again
Into the tiny, packed-tight shells.
"Dry, tasteless groundnuts," he said.
"But so easy to eat," I answered.
He lifted his hammer again and struck.
It was growing late. I continued
My walk down the long winding road.
The peanuts were like cotton in my mouth.

Sunset at Lowry

They deck with white streamers
    The high blue,
Cavort on rigid wings,
And prank the Colorado sky
    With dance.
Beneath them the sun's red flatness
Burns away the tumbled clouds
    Like a rolling prairie fire;
Then homeward at dusk
    They skim the world
While below their wings
    Groundlings grope
In the dying light.

Jet Flight

I break in rush the earth bounds
And climb to the clean, cool sky,
Jet sent like a shooting star
That rolls the earth with thunderdust;
Then heavenward to ice—
The slicing whip of wind
Whirling backward to sound.

Encased in a metal meteor,
My body moves, and I am one
With ship and light and time;
But space is my canopy—
And only beneath me is death,
And only beneath me is life,
And only beneath me is death,
And only beneath me—
Only beneath me . . .

Lines To a Lost Pilot

Too-brave pilot, who flew so high today
Across alfalfa fields and sweet red clover
And soared defiantly beyond the valleys
   and over
The snow-capped Rockies and the barren
   yellow clay
Of those distant plains—daring venturer
   into space.
Did you not know your measured limited
   place?

And how cold was the too-thin air beneath
   the moon?
And who was there to watch your spiraling
   fall
And hear your singing wings answer death's
   call?
Who saw the plummeting ship in fatal
   swoon?

Not we, for we stayed home and made the
   ancient cry:
"O Icarus, O Icarus, where art thou who
   flew too high?"
But none of us denied your right to try,
And one of us envied how you chose to die.

Evening Song No More

I remember
How in Viet Nam
On Saigon streets
I wandered down
Your face miraged
In the dusky swirl
Of daylight dying
And the cries of hawkers
Their babble swirling
Through the shuffling crowd,
I named you mine
And thought I heard
The small song of the evening bird
Riding above the traffic sound.

Then the SMASH
Of sound, exploding claymore,
And all was waste and pain—
And I lost you then.

Oh, Helen, no tower stands
In Ilium
From that day.

Overseas Diary

I have come to this place,
An old lover full of dreams,
But the sweat of wanting
Takes my strength like a fever,
And hallucination fills my hollow room
With shadows, teeming with rage
And the fear of night, where
Separation kills more men than guns.

I try to summon up her face,
But I remember her not.
Can it be all is fiction,
A story made up to ease
My restless discontent?
No! She is there waiting.
If I can just recall
One touch of her,
One breath of love.

I speak her name.
I whisper it clearly in the quiet
As if it were an incantation
Against the night.

But what comes bubbling up
From the tar pits of my mind?
It is a yearning as old and savage
As the first naked male
Bellowing at the flat moon
When he felt himself ensnared

By that aching loneliness
All men know
But know not they know
Until the moment comes—

It is a hunger that grapples
At my soul roots
And knifes the keen wanting
Through me
When I awake to emptiness
And the midnight of my bed.
Then I am on a dark plain
Lifting my eyes moonward,
Wrenching from my rigid throat
The cry that echoes throughout
Man's eternal dream.

But if I remember her not,
Who comes when I call?
What woman is that
Skirting my sleep-torn bed?
Whose warm breathing
Caresses my cheek?
Whose female scent
Flares my nostrils?

It is she who haunts each man,
That ragged whore of time's fierce moments,
She in loin cloth and matted hair,
Thick thighed and sagging breasts,
Casually crushing me beneath her;
And in the panic of my searching need,

When I cannot say the word,
My awkward, desperate pawing
Of that naked, giving, pliant flesh,
When what I want only
Is but to know the word,
To hear it spoken truly,
To touch tenderly the woman
Who lies captured
Deep inside that mound of flesh,
I know then she is more male than I,
I more female than she,
And I am choked with my own
Inarticulateness,
And my thick fingers fumble
While she scars me with laughter.

Then I know all is fiction,
The days, the places
Of having but not having,
The years of promises, and
The little lost seasons of our joy—
All fiction.

And I am sent down into
The blackest core
Of time's inferno,
From which I cannot return,
For I am lost without love,
And I am doomed to stumble
Through the pathless night
Of this foreign, fell land,
Forever damned by knowing
Separation kills more men than guns.

A Letter Never Written

I am dead, Virginia
Drowned in a rice paddy
But not in water
In my own blood
Shot through the throat
By a nine-year-old boy
He did not know me
Nor I him
No malice intended
Just fear and a gun
Were enough
We all have our villages to protect.

After he shot me
I stayed standing for a while
Staggering on long enough
To see him
Crouching, holding the rifle
Too large for him
His eyes held mine for a moment
And the world stopped
But there was no communication
As I fell foward, strangling
My M-1 automatic rifle chattered
A language we both knew
Stitched holes in the sky, the boy, the water
And we found a comradeship in death
It was all we had to share.

An Incident of Spring

On that Easter afternoon
With the smell of moist earth
Turned by my uncle's plow
To put the seed in
Strong in the warm air
My cousin took me
Behind the chicken house
Because she was older
And if I wanted to be in the game
I had to do what she told me to do
And I did
But she should not have done it
What she made me   because such things
Should not be done   for such things
Should not be   but are   but are
Oh   my aunt would have been
Screaming angry if she had known
And the preacher would have been
Most soul-shaken shocked
And my mother dead would have
Lying in her grave   cried
In the dirt and the worms

And I thought of it   so deep ashamed
I wanted to run and hide   Oh   Cousin

But there in the April day
Behind the chicken house
With the smell of hen droppings
Heavy in the soft warm air
And the sleepy clucking of setting hens
Hatching eggs in straw nests
Sounding in the quiet afternoon
So lazy and contemplative
And my cousin's laugh
I did not run   could not
And wanting   not wanting
Then dying   knowing the moment
Knowing her   losing myself
Forever bound by her whispered order
Never to tell a soul   never   never

And all summer I walked
Alone by the creek   far from my aunt's house
Across the pasture where new calves were kept
Locked from their mothers   their bellows
Following me like a memory
And I was full all season
Of a deep and haunting sorrow

And I have hated the smell
Of a chicken house   ever since

Letter to the Editor

I am no Hamlet
Fearing dreams,
But still I stay.

I get up each morning
With old expectations
Clouding my mind,
But then coffee reality
Brings me back
To radio news
And the morning paper,
With the same fruit juice
And eggs on a greasy plate
And the day ahead
Just like the last one.

I pack my lunch
In a brown paper bag
And take the bus to work,
Punch the clock,
Turn on the machine,
Open my tool box,
And sell my sweat
By the hour.

When it is over
I go home again

Through the fumes and noise
Of traffic and chatter
To find the evening
Same as the last one.

I have no great grief to bear,
No foully murdered father
To avenge,
No Queen mother to despise,
No Ophelia to bring me flowers
And madness,
Only a few tattered memories
And restless dreams
To fester in my secret soul.

But still I stay,
And I think some Monday
Or Tuesday morning,
When the weather and season
Seem right for it,
I will blow this goddamned
Routine world sky high
And leave more bodies
On the stage
Than Prince Hamlet
Ever dreamed of.

My Father Died Laughing

My father died
Laughing,
A drink in his hand
And a joke on his lips.
He knew, I think,
Better than any of us
What a slapstick,
Pratfall, burlesque,
Dirty joke
Kind of world
We live in,
And he left it,
A winner at last,
The sound of his laugh
Still rocking the foundation
When his heart stopped.

He was a poker player,
So maybe Death took a hand
And called him when he thought
He was bluffing,
But my father showed him
Four aces.
Oh, wow!
No wonder he laughed.
I wish I could have seen
The look on Death's face.

Maybe, as they say,
The best time to die
Is while you are praying,

Asking for forgiveness.
But I guess the next best
Is to be caught laughing.
And in my father's case,
His laugh was a sort of prayer,
Letting God know he wasn't complaining,
And there really wasn't much
That needed forgiving.
In fact, I think it might be
His world had to beg him for pardon.
If so, I'm sure he gave it.
He was that kind of a man,
Never could hold a grudge,
Went through life trying
To be everybody's friend,
Loving all people,
Except, perhaps, himself.
Maybe, after all, it was not
His world that did the asking,
But he ended up asking himself.
In which case, the laugh
Was his answer.
He never cared much
For self-pity.

I'm only sorry he didn't
Get to finish his drink.
It was good bourbon,
And he wasn't one
To leave a glass
Half full,
But he did.

Overheard in the Lobby
Between Double Features

What happened?
According to the old movies,
The good guys win.
Always every Saturday afternoon
Riding in
Hell for leather
Guns blazing
Hoot Gibson, Ken Maynard, Hop-along—
They wore white hats
And everybody knew,
Every popcorn-crunching,
Greasy-handed one of us knew,
They were on the side of right,
Punishing evil tirelessly,
Winning every time.

I played the game,
Paid my dues,
Served my time,
Took my licks,
Kissed my horse
Instead of the girl,
Rode right in, guns blazing.

I got clobbered!
What went wrong?
Who changed the script?
How come the good guys
Don't win anymore?

It'll Probably Be Like That

Good old what's-his-name
Doing his own thing
In the whatcha-may-call-it
Never knew the world would end
When he pulled the chain,
But it did.
Came down SPLAT on his head,
The whole damned thing.

Handy Snack

How all occasions do conspire against me
To prove my unfitness for these technocratic times.
This simple package of peanut-butter crackers
Proclaims, "Easy opening. Lift cellophane and tear."
I try with one hand, then two, scratching, clawing
Until my fingernails are broken and I know
Were my heart pure and I had the strength of ten,
I could **not** lift that cellophane and tear.
I attack with butcher knife the obdurate glassine.
Oh, bloody ruin! My wounded thumb drops gouts of
        blood
While the stubborn package remains intact,
But I will not be thwarted forever.
My hunger for the tasty morsels has grown
With every humiliating defeat. I must have them.
I put the package to my mouth and bite,
Twisting the obstinate material and pulling
Until in triumph I feel something give way.
It is my front tooth.
Now my wrath knows no bounds.
I rush into my workshop, fully equipped for the handy
        man.
Remembering my bleeding thumb, I abjure jigsaw and
        electric drill.
I take in hand cold chisel and hammer.
A few well placed blows and the package surrenders.
Never mind the crackers are now reduced to crumbs,.
I have won. The delectable morsels are mine!
I lift a cupped palmful to trembling lips
And find that they are stale.

Summer Cruise

I am going into the Bermuda Triangle,
Right through the heart of it
With all my mistakes packed in plastic bags,
Every stupid failure, misdeed, unkept promise
To my name.
Then when I disappear without a trace—
No debris floating on the water,
Not even an oil slick of shame,
Nothing left but maybe the shred of a bitter memory
In the scavenger beak of a passing sea gull—
Somebody or something somewhere,
Wherever people and things go
In the Bermuda Triangle,
Is going to get me and more garbage
Than was bargained for.
And I'll leave behind the few good things
I did and the little prizes I won
So everybody can remember me fondly.
I think it's the least I can do
For justice.

My Catch

Out into that shameless sea
Where sometimes men are prone to fish,
I tossed my net by chance,
Not expecting much, if anything,
Would find my net—it was only a weekend diversion.
I waited, amused by my waiting,
Watching the sun slide down;
Then feeling the drag grow heavy,
I hoisted the dripping web,
Thinking any fish or scuttling crab
Would bring me luck.
But the white, white skin
Glistening in the slanted sunlight
Was like no fish I'd ever known.
Then her arms dangling through the weave,
Her pale, pale hair plastering her breasts,
Her long smooth neck arched back,
Her quiet, almost serene, face turning
Toward me and her blank eyes
Staring fishlike, accusing.
I thought a nude woman drowned at sea,
Somebody's beloved tossed overboard in a storm,
Until I saw she had no legs
And the giant fish tail swaying
Was not a companion catch.
Then I dropped the net to water level

To see if she would swim,
But her only movement was the motion
Of the water slapping against my boat.
"Are you alive?" I called.
Her pink lips seemed to move,
But I heard no sound
Other than the wind ruffling the water.
In the current her arms drifted out
And one hand seemed to flutter.
I thought of the reward awaiting me at port
If I should bring her in.
"If you are dead, I might as well haul you up,"
I shouted and reached to crank the net.
Suddenly she flopped in the water,
Her huge tail slapping the rim of the net.
Then as I watched, helpless to stop her,
She climbed over the edge and dropped
Into the open water.
She surfaced once further out
And I thought she smiled and waved,
But it could have been just the sunset
Reflecting on the choppy water.

I have gone back many times
But have cast my net in vain.
It's just as well, I guess.
One mermaid in a man's life
Is more than he deserves.

Genesis III

In this dream
I went back in time
To the beginning.
It was morning and the dawn was feeble,
Sending out hesitant light
As if it wasn't quite sure yet
How it was supposed to work.
There was the Northern Cross
Still burning as if God had
Forgotten to turn off the lights,
And there was a tall mountain
Rising up black and cold
In the misty daylight dawn,
And there were gradual sounds
Of things stirring, birds chirping,
The sleepy cough of an animal,
Something moving in the brush.
Then I thought I heard weeping,
A woman weeping,
And soon I saw her nude
Coming out of an apple grove.
"Oh, Eve," I called, "have you?"
She turned, startled, gave me a look,
Then ran back among the trees.
Her sobs quivered on the morning air
And clutched me like frantic arms.
Then I knew what she had learned
From eating the fruit of the tree.
Poor Eve. Poor me. Poor everybody.

Three Coeds Walk Abreast

Three coeds walk abreast
In time to their own music
Lilting talk, treble laughter
Tumbling on the evening air
Following like a playful breeze
Their quick strides.

I stand ignored in quiet shadows
While they bounce, swish skirts
Bubble exuberance for
Some secret they will not share
Toss their heads and prance
Like nervous ponies on parade
Beat time to the melody
With clipping heels on hollow pavement.

They pass me by in chorus
Quickly move on
Then turn the corner
Fade into silence
And I am left
With only imagined echoes
Of their music.

Identity

The mirror lies.
I cannot be that one,
That product of silvered glass,
Metallic frame,
Subsisting on fluorescent light,
Streaming electrons from glass tubes,
Who grins at me out of slick brightness.
He has no blood, feels no pain, thinks no thoughts,
Loves no one.
He prances in his metallic cage,
Makes parody of my pain,
Mocks my reality
In impertinent glass,
Lies outrageously,
Says I'm ugly, old.
He pots my belly,
Thins my hair,

Doubles my chin,
Wrinkles my face
In caricature.
He apes my movements,
Frowns, grimaces,
Ponders in practiced solemnity,
Holding behind his gaze
The sly joke of similitude.

I lift my right hand to my face,
He lifts his left to his,
The reverse of truth.
Enraged, I snap the light switch.
Then he is no more before me,
And I am myself again.
I start to turn away,
But in the dark glass I think I see
A movement there.
I stand and peer steadily,
And I see a shadow peering back.

Story on Page 12

Last night in Pleasant Park
A teen-age girl and her companion
Were killed while sitting in a parked car
She, raped and strangled
He, shot three times in the face
At close range
Police Sgt. Robert Carey said
It was the worst mess
He had ever seen
In his twenty-two years on the force
The boy's brains were splattered all over
The inside of the car
And the girl's underpants were tied
Around her throat
So tight they had to cut them off
Sgt. Carey said she was probably alive
When the boy was shot
Sitting beside him, but she was

Too scared to move or cry out
Some of his blood and brains
Were on her shoulder and in her hair
Then the rape and afterwards
The strangulation, he thought.
The girl's name was Jennifer Smith
She would have graduated next week
From City High, salutatorian
The boy was Ken Walker, who worked for
The First National Bank, assistant cashier
"He had a bright future," President Wilford said
"Shocking," said Mayor Parker
"Something has to be done about this"
Police Chief Albright suggested
They close the park after sundown.

The Reward

What did they do for her
After eighty years of serving?
Took her from her creaking chair,
The flowered curtains wilting,
The wallpaper fading, the house
Needing paint, run-down, cluttered
With too many things she couldn't throw out,
Turned her back from the kitchen sink
Where she had spent most of her life
Washing dishes and peeling vegetables,
Put out the stove where pots had boiled
And bread browned in the ancient oven,
Turned off the lights and water,
Disconnected the telephone, stopped her mail,
Sold her furniture and dishes,
Took her '59 Chevy to the junk yard,
And let her keep only as much
As would fit into two suitcases
And her worn leather purse.

Then they took her to the nursing home,
Got her settled in a pleasant place
Where people could look out for her,
See that she ate proper food,
Got her naps regularly, bathed,
Even had her hair fixed once a month,
Provided magazines and her own TV set,
Did everything they could to make her comfortable,
Then left her.

She stayed awhile,
Gave no trouble,
Even tried to fit in,
Helping those who could not see,
Could not hear, or could not walk
As well as she;
Tried to make conversation,
Discuss the children, recipes,
Sometimes what was said on the evening news,

Gave up when she discovered
Nobody was listening,
Not even herself;
Watched from the big window
The sun, the rain, the seasons
Flow by like a silent parade;
Wrote a few letters in her small, cramped hand,
Always careful not to bother anyone
With complaints;
Read her Bible every night;
Then slipped away when nobody was watching.

They returned to make arrangements,
Packed what was left in two suitcases
And her worn leather purse,
Thanked everyone for being so nice,
Then drove back to their own lives,
Content that they had done
All expected of them.

A Trap Untended

Sometimes an insidious mouse
Nibbles the bait away
Ever so carefully until
The trap is empty and unsprung.
Left cocked and waiting,
It holds only expectancy,
Kept by hope,
The rusting spring coiled
Taut against the trigger,
Waiting to catch something—
Anything that will spring it—
Wanting to be what it is,
To do what it was made to do,
To realize itself,
But the mouse has stolen the cheese
A little at a time in petty bites
And left the trap empty,
Unfulfilled,
Wondering what it is for,
Why it was put there
Only to be ignored
By the one who set it,
Until out of its own despair
It finds the strength to hurl its challenge
At the universe—
One protest, a SNAP—
Then embraces itself
In the hollow silence
Of nothing caught.

He Spent Too Long

He spent too long
Window shopping
Learning the ropes
Standing outside doors
Arriving late
Leaving early
Missing the point
Ignoring the question
Checking the rules
Considering consequences
Counting his change
Preparing for action.

Now it is way past noon
And the late sun falls
Too swiftly down a pale sky
Toward a pastel sunset
His shadow lengthens
He hears the plaintive coo of a single dove
Shivers in the cooling dusk
His worn coat buttoned close
He hesitates to go in.

Once too young
Now too old
He stands in the darkening day
Fearing their laughter.

Siesta
(For one who died as gently as he lived.)

Outside his open window, silence
In soft afternoon garden where
An ignorant bee droned dulcet song
Hummed drowsy among the honeysuckle
Gathered sweet droplets of nectar
And drugged the heavy-eyed patriarch
Until sleep stole his life away
One breath at a time.

On Reflection

We have come a distance
In our geographical game
I searching, it hiding
In strange ports
The elusive something
Discreetly waiting just beyond
The edge of light
I always thought, fully expected
That I would someday somewhere
But it is late now
I feel like I arrived at the restaurant
And found the bus boys stacking chairs
I got to the circus and found
The roustabouts taking down the tent

I reached the station just in time
To watch the last train pull out.

Maybe it has something to do with the fact
That I was born on Wednesday, full of woe.

I had envisioned somewhere a place
But I was always a stranger
Just passing through, never unpacking
Forever arriving the day after
Finding familiar landscapes in foreign lands
Suffering nostalgia when I came home
Experiencing deja vu in unfamiliar locales
But nobody else knew their lines.

It seems that the game is ending now
And I look back in sadness
At the missing part never found
I guess there were too many paths in the forest
And the birds ate all my crumbs.

Odysseus To Penelope

I return to you, old wife,
With blood on my hands—
My blood,
And on my cheeks—
My tears,
And in my heart—
My pain.

I bring no other trophies
From those twenty long years
Of wars and wanderings
In the hands of capricious gods,
Except myself, worn and scarred.

I greet you untriumphant
And stand in awe of your adamantine spirit
That kept your chastity unblemished
In the weave of an unfinished shroud.
I bow to your virtue, good wife,
And ask, for the sake of my crimes,
Permission to kneel before you.
Accept with grace my contrition,
And grant me entrance to that closed chamber
Where I may find salvation
In your tenacious love.

The Promise

Winter brings a promise
To those who can endure.
Like the trick memory plays,
Making the dream
Possess the dreamer,
Saying all before was better,
Winter whispers, "Will be."

I, alone, listen sleepily,
Caught between promise and memory,
Hearing the soft swish of snow
Across the windowed wall,
Like the sighs of restless children
Waiting for love and magic
Packaged in bright colors,
Forever captured in the slow fall
Of snow flakes, sifting down,
The dead white of time mounding
Over the bodies of lost friends, old loves.

The cold is outside, embracing them
In their bundled joy of snow play,

Laughter in the wind, but ice pellets
Slap their faces until they weep.
I could have told them there is no love
In a freezing wind. But they would not have listened.

Inside, I am warmed by the burning logs
Dancing frail shadows on the ceiling
In time with the castanet snaps
Of flames eating up the hard timber
Of my dead father's summer land.
Its wavering circle of heat holds back
The chill that skirts just beyond,
And I am secure within the circle,
So I sit, slumped in half-sleep,
Pretended ease, in my heavy,
Black leather chair.

Enthroned like an old false god
By innocents, I await their chattering return,
Driven back to me in time by sleet and wind,
Their young voices bubbling over
With the promise they bring
Out of that dark December day.

In Answer to Your Question

What is poetry?
It is movement
The flowing out
From me to you
The flowing back
From you to me
Of sound and sense
Through language
Controlled
An experience of experience
Shared in time
Through time
Something perishable preserved
Caught, fixed, held
For a while in print
A quiet melody replayed
Echoing in a mute chamber
After the music maker has gone
A prayer, a confession,
A self-lecture, a dream,
A hope repeated.
It is, finally, a kind of love affair
A poet has with his world
When he can get someone
To listen.

Closing Scene

Beyond the curtained window
I see the dull night, layered in shadows,
A thin red light streaks the breaking sky,
Coruscating a crescent hill like dawn,
Or maybe it is the last touch of sunset—
I have no sense of time in this place,
Only the slow movement of change,
The going out and coming in like breath.

Somewhere a ceaseless ocean rolls
And I am beached like a spent swimmer,
Gasping for air wheezing through fatal tubes,
And too tired to lift a limp arm
Or move a soggy, leadened leg, I wait.
Then a racking cough wrenches me in pain,
Followed by a merciful, warm release.

No more the clock, the clink of coins,
The expectation dashed, the truth realized.

Now that crimson stretch of sky is all,
And worlds revolve around me
While the bee hum of existence swirls
Like a twisting wind slowly spiraling down,
And I am its vortex, the still eye of calm
Around which the dark attendants move,
The point upon which all lines converge,
The alpha and omega of something fragile
Caught, held, fixed for a moment,
At the apex of its climb
Before the roller coaster starts down—

Ah, friends, had I but time
I could tell you of the dream,
The dream unfinished—now ended—
Now begun . . .